Constitution Day

Crabtree Publishing Company

www.crabtreebooks.com

Crabtree Publishing Company
www.crabtreebooks.com

Author: Molly Aloian
Coordinating editor: Chester Fisher
Series editor: Susan Labella
Project manager: Kavita Lad (Q2AMEDIA)
Art direction: Dibakar Acharjee (Q2AMEDIA)
Cover design: Ranjan Singh (Q2AMEDIA)
Design: Tarang Saggar (Q2AMEDIA)
Photo research: Sakshi Saluja (Q2AMEDIA)
Editor: Kelley MacAulay
Copy editor: Adrianna Morganelli
Proofreader: Crystal Sikkens
Project coordinator: Robert Walker
Production coordinator: Katherine Kantor
Font management: Mike Golka
Prepress technicians: Samara Parent, Ken Wright

Photographs:
Cover: Associated Press, J. Helgason/Shutterstock
(background); Title page: Blend Images/Jupiter
Images; P4: Joshua Haviv/Istockphoto; P5: Big Cheese
Photo/Jupiter Images; P7: Coston Stock/Alamy; P9:
Jani Bryson/Istockphoto; P10: Lisafx/Dreamstime;
P11: Geom/Shutterstock; P13: Drbueller/Istockphoto;
P15: Hulton Archive/Getty images; P16: Jeremy
Edwards/Istockphoto; P17: DoD media; P18: Bonnie
Jacobs/Istockphoto; P19: Daaronj/Istockphoto;
P21: Tetra Images/Jupiter Images; P23: Stefanie
Timmermann/Istockphoto; P24: Associated Press;
P27: Stanislav Khrapov/Shutterstock; P28:
Thinkstock Images/Jupiter Images; P29: Glenda
Powers/Dreamstime; P31: Peter Titmuss/Alamy

Library and Archives Canada Cataloguing in Publication

Aloian, Molly
    Constitution Day / Molly Aloian.

(Celebrations in my world)
Includes index.

ISBN 978-0-7787-4286-9 (bound).--ISBN 978-0-7787-4304-0 (pbk.)

    1. Constitution Day (U.S.)--Juvenile literature. 2. United States.
Constitution--Anniversaries, etc.--Juvenile literature. I. Title. II. Series.

E303.A46 2008   j394.264'0973   C2008-903486-4

Library of Congress Cataloging-in-Publication Data

Aloian, Molly.
  Constitution Day / Molly Aloian
    p. cm. -- (Celebrations in my world)
  Includes index.
  ISBN-13: 978-0-7787-4304-0 (pbk. : alk. paper)
  ISBN-10: 0-7787-4304-7 (pbk. : alk. paper)
  ISBN-13: 978-0-7787-4286-9 (reinforced library binding : alk. paper)
  ISBN-10: 0-7787-4286-5 (reinforced library binding : alk. paper)
  1. Constitution Day (U.S.)--Juvenile literature. 2. United States. Constitution-
-Anniversaries, etc.--Juvenile literature. 3. United States--Politics and
government--1783-1789--Juvenile literature. 4. Constitutional history--United
States--Juvenile literature. I. Title. II. Series.

E303.A46 2009
320.973--dc22
                           2008023531

Crabtree Publishing Company
www.crabtreebooks.com   1-800-387-7650

Published in Canada
Crabtree Publishing
616 Welland Ave.
St. Catharines, ON
L2M 5V6

Published in the United States
Crabtree Publishing
PMB16A
350 Fifth Ave., Suite 3308
New York, NY 10118

Published in the United Kingdom
Crabtree Publishing
White Cross Mills
High Town, Lancaster
LA1 4XS

Published in Australia
Crabtree Publishing
386 Mt. Alexander Rd.
Ascot Vale (Melbourne)
VIC 3032

Contents

What is It?

Constitution Day is an American holiday. On this day, the United States **Constitution** was approved. Americans celebrate this event! The United States Constitution is the written document that sets up the **supreme** law and government of the United States of America. So, Constitution Day is the birthday of the United States government!

The Statue of Liberty stands for freedom and **democracy**.

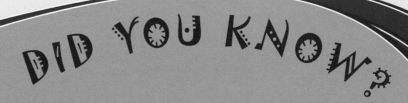

DID YOU KNOW?

Constitution Day is a federal holiday. A federal holiday is a national holiday, which is celebrated throughout the United States. Others are Memorial Day and Columbus Day.

To celebrate Constitution Day, some children recite the **Pledge of Allegiance.**

When is It?

Constitution Day is September 17. On September 17, 1787, the U.S. Constitutional Convention signed the Constitution. A Constitutional Convention is a gathering of people who work together to agree on the laws for a country. Many people believe that Constitution Day is just as important as Independence Day. It's a time to celebrate the birth of the United States government! Many people believe this government is the greatest form of government ever known.

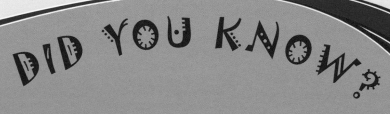

DID YOU KNOW?

On April 15, 1957, the City Council of Louisville, Ohio declared the city Constitution Town.

The first three words in the **Preamble** to the Constitution are "We the people ..."

Who Celebrates?

Constitution Day is a day to celebrate being an American citizen! It is celebrated throughout the United States by all American citizens. Some American citizens were born in the United States, whereas others became American citizens after they moved to the United States. Families celebrate the day at home and teachers and children celebrate the day at school.

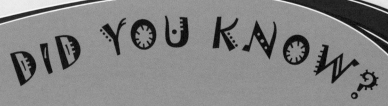

DID YOU KNOW?

The U.S. Constitution is 4,400 words long. It contains seven articles, or pieces of writing. It is the oldest and shortest constitution of any major government in the world.

These children are all American citizens. Some were born in the United States. Others came to the United States from other countries.

An Important Day!

People celebrate Constitution Day because they want everyone to know it is an important day. The Constitution provides the people of America with rights and freedoms. These rights include the right to vote for the leaders of the government.

● This woman is voting.

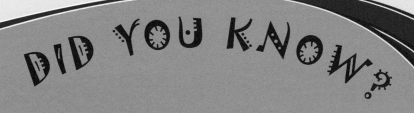

DID YOU KNOW?

Constitution Day was once called "Citizenship Day." In 2004, the day was renamed Constitution Day.

People celebrate because they want to protect and defend the Constitution and their own rights as American citizens. By celebrating this day in U.S. history, people can also teach others about the Constitution and the rights all people should have.

This boy is learning about his rights as an American citizen.

The History

In 1787, **representatives** from 12 states formed the Constitutional Convention. They spent nearly four months in Philadelphia writing the Constitution. The representatives included George Washington, Benjamin Franklin, and James Madison. They discussed and **debated** many ideas while writing the document. The document was written so that the duties, or jobs, of the government and the duties of each state were separate.

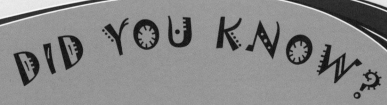

DID YOU KNOW?

On May 13, 1787, George Washington rode into Philadelphia to attend the Federal Convention. The Convention was held in what is known today as Independence Hall.

The Constitution explains how the representatives of the people should be elected, or chosen.

In 1787, this building was called the Pennsylvania State House. This is where the Declaration of Independence was signed on July 4, 1776. Today, it is called Independence Hall.

Signing

The Constitution was signed in September of 1787. **Congress** then sent copies to the state legislatures for approval. The state legislatures are elected representatives of the people. Some state legislatures approved of the Constitution, whereas others did not. After much debate and discussion, the Constitution finally was approved. This document would govern, or control and manage, democracy in America!

DID YOU KNOW?

Many people believe that the Constitution is a good example of cooperation and compromise. For it to be written and approved, people had to work together.

Senator Robert Byrd encourages all Americans to learn about the Constitution.

Learning About It

Each year, on September 17, every school and college that receives federal money, or money from the government, must teach students about the Constitution. Each school can decide what kind of educational program they will use to teach students about the Constitution on this day.

● There are many books you can read to learn about the Constitution.

These students are working on a Constitution Day project.

Teachers can use different and creative ways to help students learn about this important document.

DID YOU KNOW?

When Constitution Day falls on a weekend or on another holiday, schools must schedule a teaching program immediately before or after September 17.

Take a Trip!

There are many ways to celebrate Constitution Day. One way to celebrate is to take a trip to see the document! Each year, hundreds of thousands of people visit Washington, D.C., to see the original copy of the United States Constitution. It is on display at the National Archives. The National Archives is a place that protects documents and materials created by the United States government.

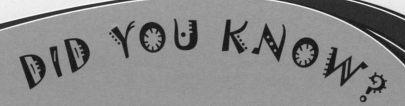

DID YOU KNOW?

The Public Vaults is an exhibit at the National Archives. **Historical** *documents and photos are displayed there. Each exhibit's theme is based on words from the Constitution's Preamble.*

Admission to the National Archives is free and the original Constitution is on display there. You get to see it in person!

This picture shows a copy of the United States Constitution.

City Celebrations

Some cities hold National Constitution Day celebrations. During these celebrations, people can see and enjoy many fun events. There are public readings of the Constitution, during which parts of the Constitution are read out loud for an audience. The audience is sometimes asked to take part! Face-painting, special music, and fireworks are also part of some celebrations. All of these things are meant to remind people of how important Constitution Day is. Celebrating with friends, family, and your community is a way to honor and **commemorate** the United States Constitution!

This girl has her face painted
for Constitution Day.

Watch It!

People must raise their right hands when they take their oath of citizenship.

Another way to celebrate Constitution Day is to observe, or watch, a swearing-in ceremony for new U.S. citizens. During this ceremony, people become U.S. citizens by taking an oath of citizenship. An oath is a kind of promise. One of the things they promise is to support and defend the Constitution. Watching one of these ceremonies reminds people that the Constitution is important to all U.S. citizens. In order to be granted, or given, U.S. citizenship, **foreign** citizens must go through a process called **naturalization**. To complete the process, people must do several things. Some of these things include living in the United States for a specific amount of time, being able to read, write, and speak English, and knowing and understanding American history.

25

Walk It!

To celebrate Constitution Day and learn more about where the Constitution was created, some people go on the Constitutional Walking Tour of Philadelphia. The tour includes visits to the most popular historic sites in Philadelphia. You can take a free self-guided tour, a guided tour, or a group tour. The National Constitution Center, Independence Hall, the Liberty Bell Center, and the National Liberty Museum are some of the sites you could visit.

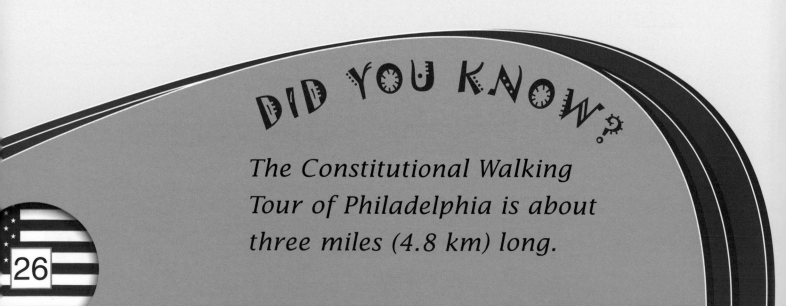

DID YOU KNOW?

The Constitutional Walking Tour of Philadelphia is about three miles (4.8 km) long.

The building in this picture is called Library Hall.

Red, White, and Blue

These girls are making a Constitution Day poster with red and blue markers.

DID YOU KNOW?

You can make a Constitution Day crossword puzzle or quiz to give to your friends and family.

You can have your own Constitution Day celebration! Visit your local library and look for books about the Constitution. Invite your friends to a Constitution Day party. In honor of the day, you can serve red, white, and blue foods and drinks. You can make red, white, and blue posters or bulletin boards to hang up for Constitution Day. You can even wear red, white, and blue clothing to show your American spirit! Ask your parents if there are any Constitution Day celebrations such as parades or concerts in your community and make plans to attend with your friends and family.

• This girl is wearing red, white, and blue.

Learning More!

Learn more about the Constitution and why it is so important to celebrate Constitution Day. Visit www.constitutionfacts.com and test your Constitution I.Q. On this website, you will find crossword puzzles, treasure hunts, word finds, famous quotes, important dates to remember, and a fascinating facts quiz. Once you know your Constitution I.Q., you can challenge your friends and family by playing a question and answer game. You can even keep score!

DID YOU KNOW?

There are pocket-sized copies of the Constitution available at www.constitutionfacts.com.

Ask your friends and family to complete
a Constitution Day crossword puzzle
that you have created.

Glossary

admission The price of entrance

commemorate To remember and mark with a ceremony

Congress The main lawmakers in the United States, including the Senate and the House of Representatives

constitution The document that lays out the laws according to which a country is governed

debate To discuss a problem in a formal way

democracy A system of government in which people select those who will run the country

foreign Describing someone from another country

historical Relating to history

naturalization The process by which a person becomes an American citizen

pledge of allegiance The promise that a person will follow the laws of the country

preamble An introduction

representatives People who serve as agents for others

senator A member of the Senate

supreme Highest in rank or authority

Index

Printed in the U.S.A.